ISIS:

The Islamic Terrorist Signals Armageddon is HERE

THE FINAL BATTLE OF GOOD VS. EVIL HAS BEGUN

NANCY TAYLOR

WESTBOW
P R E S S®
A DIVISION OF THOMAS NELSON
& ZONDERVAN

WestBow Press books may be ordered through booksellers or by contacting:

WestBow Press
A Division of Thomas Nelson & Zondervan
1663 Liberty Drive
Bloomington, IN 47403
www.westbowpress.com
1 (866) 928-1240

ISBN: 978-1-5127-2892-7 (sc)
ISBN: 978-1-5127-2894-1 (hc)
ISBN: 978-1-5127-2893-4 (e)

Library of Congress Control Number: 2016901620

Print information available on the last page.

WestBow Press rev. date: 02/04/2016

Dedication

To my Father

Preface

Dear Reader,

It is with great concern and love for all of God's people that we be saved in these End Times we face. We can see the prophets in the ancient times and see that the warnings of Jesus Christ are being fulfilled before our very eyes: nuclear bombs capable of destroying one-third of the world within one hour, beheadings of Christians, fleeing refugees, and a world drunk with lawlessness.

It is critical that we take heed to the Word of God for in it we will be able to overcome all the fiery darts from our adversary.

The End Times refer to spiritual attacks, especially to Christianity and our faith in Christ.

We cannot ignore God's Word, and it is with prayer that this book will bring you closer to God and understanding through the Holy Spirit. Then your spiritual eyes will be opened to edify, strengthen, and encourage you to be the person God created you to be, one body in Christ.

Acknowledgments

I wish to thank the following who helped make my book a reality:

Lee Barnathan, my editor.

Lee, thank you for being a second set of eyes for this manuscript when I couldn't see my own work after reading it so many times. Thank you for your diligence and research to ensure the Scripture quotations are correct and for the time you took to ensure the quality of this book wasn't compromised. You're appreciated!

WestBow Press Team

Thank you all for your efforts in helping to put this book together.

From the coordinator, editorial, and design—what a feat! Also, the Christian values are what I appreciate in knowing this book was in good hands.

Above all, this book acknowledges the brave men, women, and children who have suffered persecution for having faith in Christ. May your testimonies be an encouragement for us to continue to fight the good fight in our faith in Christ. Then we may overcome and be victorious as you have and endure to the end.

May God bless all of you. Thank you from the bottom of my heart.

The Bible has two parts: the Old Testament and the New Testament. The Old Testament explains how good and evil evolved into this world, beginning with Adam and Eve. With them there was no knowledge of good and evil; however evil existed before man and tried to do what it knows best: to seek and destroy God's plans.

The New Testament is the birth of Jesus Christ, and He explains in Revelation how evil will be finally destroyed and what we need to know and be prepared for. Prior to that great day of tribulation, many will be tested and faced with evil regarding their faith in God.

These aspects of the Bible, for many of us, can be difficult to understand, and many of us give up or misinterpret its meaning.

This is unfortunate, for there are significant messages God wants us to know for our own good so we are prepared for the End Times.

I have set out to help clarify key words and phrases Jesus used to help us understand what we need to know so these tools can help us overcome the challenges we face today.

Good and evil are the basic forces we are familiar with, but at times it is hard to understand where or why some of us are born with them.

Good and evil are as real as the spirits that rule them. They have been around since when God threw Satan out of heaven, and is the same ruling force today.

I ask myself, as I am aware that many others will ask the same, "How can God allow such a Beast to enter our world and not stop it?" It is a puzzling question, as are many we have, but this is where I feel it is essential for us to study and understand the Word of God. Then we can see the whole picture.

It is important to know that there is a divine plan since the beginning of time, and nothing happens without God's knowledge.

God is a loving God who allows us free will or freedom of choice, but he will warn us, as he did in Genesis 2:17. God said, "Of the tree of the knowledge of good and evil you shall not eat, for in the day you eat of it you shall surely die."

This is why it is necessary to be careful in the choices we make today, but let me stay on point here. God never tempts us to sin (James 1:13). Satan does the tempting. I can think of five purposes God has if we choose God's way over our own.

1. The power of free will. Although God has total control, he also wants you to be able to make your own decisions, even though he knows what choices you will make.

   He already knew what Eve was going to do, even though He had warned her. This is why God had already prepared Jesus even before the foundations of the world. God created Jesus to be our Savior and to be born in flesh for the future.

2. Edification for growth and wisdom. Without pain we wouldn't truly understand happiness.

3. Spiritual cleansing as God foresaw the final hour of Satan's last day

4. Jesus's entering and bringing wisdom of the End Times

5. God's separation of good and evil for good

Now, all this may sound elementary, but we need to start with the foundation to get to the core of where we are today.

Even though God knew we would choose to sin, as a loving God he also provided us a way to escape.

The New Testament begins with Jesus's birth. He defeated death with his sacrifice at Calvary. Jesus's birth occurred to separate sin from his people, to be the bridge for those who chose to cross over from death to life.

When the Son of God entered our world, he did so with conviction, determination, and love through the Holy Spirit to help unbelievers, sinners, and believers understand God's loving plan overall.

Even many high priests were misguided and have misinterpreted the Old Testament and left out some of the most important messages God wanted us to know—namely, love and forgiveness to one another, not an eye for an eye. Because the people living in those ancient times didn't have true atonement for their sins, many lived in a sinful lifestyle and couldn't comprehend Scripture the way it was meant to be read.

Jesus came to teach them and future generations the consequence of sin. At the same time, Jesus came and conquered sin through his death and became the true atonement for our sins through our belief in him.

One of Jesus's last words on the cross was to God, asking for forgiveness for his murderers. Luke 23:34 says, "Then said Jesus, Father, forgive them; for they know not what they do." That was the ultimate love and sacrifice Jesus gave to his Father for our sins.

Jesus prayed for love and forgiveness, even for those who were lost and brutally murdered him.

There is spiritual power in these two elements that not only free you from bondage but also release you from Satan's hatred and revenge for God's people.

For your own good, any opportunity you have to forgive anyone who has done you harm actually gives you power. This is not for the one who harmed you, unless he or she comes to repentance, which would be very therapeutic for you to pray for.

However, God is a God of justice, and he will be the final judge. We don't need to worry about justice for the harm the offender caused us, because God knows everything and has the last vengeance.

Rather, forgive so you can be free. For God even said, "It would be better for him if a millstone were hung around his neck, and he were thrown into the sea, than that he should offend ..." (Luke 17:2)

Spiritual punishment is far more painful. It is internal, severe, and longer than any physical punishment one can experience, regardless of how much torture people can inflict on others. However, God is slow to anger and does not wish harm on anyone. He wants everyone to have a chance to be saved and to come to repentance, since He knows there is a final hour when that door will be shut forever.

Jesus constantly reminded people of the negative spiritual impact of condemning each other and throwing guilt, shame, or the blame game as we see today. This is a tactic Satan uses; he is the great prosecutor looking for faults to condemn you with, and Satan can have an open door to cause havoc in your life, because sin separates us from God. If we learn to forgive the sins of others, we will also be forgiven, and Satan cannot touch us.

Jesus said in John 8:7, "He who is without sin among you, let him throw a stone at her first." We all have sinned and fallen short; ego can be our worst enemy, as it prevents us from experiencing spiritual enlightenment. I highly recommend that we reflect before throwing stones at anyone.

Ask yourself whether you are guilty of the same. Instead of the blame approach, let others know with kindness that they are wrong so they have an opportunity to correct it through wisdom and understanding.

People use manipulation and twist the gospel for their own benefit; this is true today, and you see preachers who look like they should actually be used-car salesmen.

For instance, some preach love for greedy purposes, twisting blessings for personal gain. These are not real blessings, for God knows the intent of the heart.

We must be willing to put God first instead of ourselves for gain, expecting Him to bless us.

Trust me, no Mercedes Benz will save you when the Enemy of your soul confronts you if you haven't placed the Word of God in your life.

God has warned us about false Christs, as God said many will preach to soothe itchy ears, meaning to get the population for their own pocket gain. This is because it's much easier to sell what you want to hear

Nancy Taylor

than what you don't. For God said, "But seek first the kingdom of God and His righteousness, and all these things shall be added to you" (Matthew 6:33).

One of the reasons we are not blessed with material gain is because we want it without doing the work. We stay in our own course while going through life, making no effort to challenge our spiritual growth, and remaining, to some degree, spiritually dead.

Studying God's Word takes work, and yes, although many ungodly men are blessed with material gain, God says, "Lay not up for yourselves treasures upon earth, where moth and rust doth corrupt, and where thieves break through and steal" (Matthew 6:19).

We need to put God first, because when we do, we will understand what is important and what isn't. We will see the world differently and know how to prioritize what is most valuable in our lives, such as family, moral values, and perseverance.

Only then can we truly enjoy what we have, having God's loving Spirit. Everything else is just icing on the cake and is so much more meaningful and enjoyable.

However, with the challenges we face today, there are more important matters to be concerned about than material gain. We need to focus more on spiritual matters, since we are in the end times. No financial gain will save us, and time is critical, so we should spend our time in spiritual preparation, for God knows all we need before we even ask.

There are so many denominations and faith-based organizations that have taught their own version of the Word of God. But those are not the true teachings. The problem with this is that they don't truly equip you for the final days, and many people are still confused because they are not truly studying Jesus's Word and his warnings of the End Times, even though they are at our front doorstep.

This is exactly what the Enemy wants to plant: seeds of confusion and a lack of the truth and knowledge of what is to come. His ultimate plan is to confuse us so we continue to go our own way, out of God's way, so he can destroy us.

Jesus came to warn us about that, and in Matthew 24:34, He said, "This generation will by no means pass away till all these things take place." This verse confirms that God knows what is going to happen step by step. No gates of hell or heaven can change it, for God knows even the numbers of every strand of hair on your head.

Yes, brothers and sisters, God is in full control. This doesn't mean we can trust Him to do everything for us, for Jesus said, "Thus also faith by itself, if it does not have works, is dead" (James 2:17). So we must do our part. We must be diligent and learn all we can to overcome these challenging times.

Jesus came to educate us and clear up man-made conceptions of traditions, such as the Sabbath day, the day of rest, considered a holy day of God.

Jesus's mission was to heal, save sinners, and bring people to repentance. For instance, on the Sabbath day, the Scribes and Pharisees knew Jesus's tender heart for the weak and the meek. They waited to see whether he would heal anyone on the Sabbath day so they could find an act to accuse him of. They wanted to find fault in him to prove he wasn't the perfect One without sin, because working on the Sabbath day was considered a sin, and they believed helping someone was work.

Take Luke 6:9, for example. Jesus said to a man who had an injured hand to stand up and come in front for all to see. Jesus knew their thoughts and said to them, "I will ask you one thing: Is it lawful on the Sabbath to do good or to do evil, to save life or to destroy?" Jesus, looking at everyone around him, told the man to stretch out his hand, and when he did, his hand was restored and healed. The Scribes and Pharisees were furious and discussed with each other what they should do to Jesus.

You see, the ignorance Jesus faced then is the same ignorance we face today. We find lack of compassion, sympathy, and love to help others. Our hearts are vexed when we put matters of this world first, and we turn a blind eye when we should extend a helping hand.

I was at Costco one day and saw a mother with a child; she was asking for money. Yes, this request can appear deplorable, since it may seem to some that she was using a child to get sympathy, but let's face it: what mother in her right mind would do that if she didn't need help?

I stayed there for an hour, and no one extended any help but passed her by. Her boy was getting tired, and you couldn't ignore the stress on his face.

There was an In-N-Out Burger across the street, and I give her money and purchased burgers, drinks, and fries for her and her boy. The boy began eating and gobbled the food up right away; it was clear that they were very hungry while standing in the sun with little shade. She was very grateful.

We really need to pay attention to our hearts, as the issue of selfishness versus selflessness is serious; the last thing you want to have is a selfish heart. If this describes you today, please repent and have the love of God in your heart, for we are far closer to harder times, and you need to be equipped for them. The only way to be prepared is through God's strength, but you can't have it if he isn't in you.

We can see how important love and charity are to God, for God is love; and it is written in Matthew 25 that when souls died and met with the Lord, he said,

> For I was hungry and you gave me nothing to eat; I was thirsty and you gave me nothing to drink, I was a stranger and you did not invite me in, I needed clothes, and you did not clothe me, I was sick and in prison and you did not look after me.
>
> They also will answer, "Lord, when did we see you hungry or thirsty or a

stranger or needing clothes or sick in prison, and did not help you"?

The Lord will reply, Truly I tell you, whatever you did not do for the least of these, you did not do for me.

Then they will go away to eternal punishment, but the righteous to eternal life. (Matthew. 25:43–46)

Then the King will say to those on His right hand, 'Come, you blessed of My Father, inherit the kingdom prepared for you from the foundation of the world: for I was hungry and you gave Me food; I was thirsty and you gave Me drink; I was a stranger and you took Me in." (Matthew 25:34–35)

God gave us a few powerful tools to keep in mind to fight the good fight, since the Enemy won't sleep until he has destroyed as many souls as possible. Remember, we are in spiritual warfare, so don't let him take your soul at all costs.

The Bible was meant for his people and for those who are lost to come to Jesus; it was not written for the Enemy, although the Enemy uses the Bible and twists the truth. But it will do no good for the Evil One, for God knows it falls on deaf ears and that the truth isn't in him.

The Bible and revelation Jesus preached about are intended to help us be prepared, as he loves us and wants us home.

God gives us his armor, and this is a tool to meditate on and memorize. As it is written in Ephesians 6:10–12, "Finally, my brethren, be strong in the Lord, and in the power of his might. Put on the whole armor of God, that you may be able to stand against the wiles of the devil. For we wrestle not against flesh and blood, but against principalities, against powers, against the rulers of the darkness of this age, against spiritual hosts of wickedness in heavenly places."

This is spiritual warfare, as the Enemy is fighting to convince you that there is no God or that you cannot trust in him. He will convince you of doubts; fear is his favorite tactic to make you feel you aren't worthy and cannot be forgiven of your failures and deception among many other lies.

He is the prosecutor and deceiver, and he will attack your mind in a crafty way to distort the truth so you will believe a lie. He searches for your faults, sins, and failures; and he will attack your mind and heart, speaking to you that you are not worthy of God's forgiveness and that you have committed a horrible act. He will make you feel guilty, condemning you and throwing obstacles until you give up hope.

Jesus said in John 8:44, "You are of your father the devil, and the desires of your father you want to do. He was a murderer from the beginning, and does not stand in the truth, because there is no truth in him. When he speaks a lie, he speaks from his own resources, for he is a liar and the father of it."

Jesus said that through him there is no condemnation, for we are saved through the grace of God through the sacrifice of Jesus Christ through his death on Calvary.

Once we repent and come to believe Jesus is our Lord and Savior, we are cleansed from *all* condemnation.

We all will continue to sin since we are not perfect; however, we must constantly fight the enemy through the faith we have in Christ. This is our shield.

Once we remember and take to heart these fundamental principles -- that Christ died for us, that we should repent, that we are saved through the grace of God – then we can be prepared to march forward into the great battle of that evil day many Christians have faced and are facing now. They will face persecution in the near future.

It is essential to understand what each of these spiritual principles represents in nature as we engage in spiritual warfare; after all, this is what the Enemy is after: our souls. Therefore, it is written in Ephesians 6:14–18 that we should have the armor of God as follows.

1. Gird your waist with truth. This means to hold yourself together with truth, which is the opposite of lies, and remain in reality of facts. God is One, and there is no other; this is the truth. Jesus is our Lord and Savior, and through him we are saved; this is the truth. Satan has a short time before he will be sent forever to hell and will have no power over you; this is the truth. Satan will always try his tactics to deceive you and confuse you with lies and doubts; it's important to know the truth so you don't believe a lie and are deceived.

2. Put on the breastplate of righteousness. God gives us his shield of righteousness to protect

our inner organs, such as our hearts, which Satan loves to attack. This is a spiritual shield of God's righteousness we should put on and call on when attacked. Standing for what's right is far better than standing for what's wrong. The Enemy will try to tempt you into doing something wrong and get you off God's track.

3. Stand with your feet firm in the gospel of peace, which we will use to show God's image in all we do. If you speak peacefully, there is no ill word Satan can use against you.

4. Take the helmet of salvation, which is Christ who died for you and purchased you with his blood. You are an heir of the kingdom of God. This is knowing without a shadow of a doubt that Jesus died for your sins and that Satan cannot take that away from you. Your sins are forgiven.

5. Take the sword of the Spirit, which is the Word of God, always praying and asking God for help in doing His will. God's Word is stronger than any double-edged sword. It will cut through any deception.

6. Above all, take the shield of faith, with which you will be able to quench all the fiery darts of the Wicked One.

Faith is the opposite of doubt, which cannot and will not penetrate your heart, mind, and soul as long as you keep the faith. Faith is believing in the unseen, knowing God is there. The stronger your belief, the better you are able to reject Satan's attacks. Do not give up hope and faith, as hard as it may be, for the day of the Lord is coming.

There is no question that there have been countless battles and wars in all of history, as Jesus predicted. "And you will hear of wars and rumors of wars. See that you are not troubled; for all these things must come to pass, but the end is not yet. For nation will rise against nation, and kingdom against kingdom. And there will be famines, pestilences, and earthquakes in various places. (Matthew 24:6–7).

Many believe this is history repeating itself, but Jesus said in Matthew 24:8, "All these are the beginning of sorrows." Each stage will get worse, harder, stronger, faster.

Also, the difference is that technology we have today brings awareness that the monstrosity we witness, such as 9/11, is far worse than ever before. Evil is able to use technology for far worse damage, and it will get worse until the world will be at the worst state it has ever been.

The fascinating part of all this is that we are witnessing God's prophecy; we are part of his plan, and each of us is accountable for our part and role in all of history. That's pretty significant, and it's scary.

Regardless of what happens now or tomorrow, we must always stand for the truth and for God, even if it costs our lives. I will get more into this later as we head into the great battle of Armageddon.

First, you need to be equipped and ready, as the End Times is sooner than later. This is a time to be bold and stronger than ever before within yourself and your relationship with God.

However, those who are strong will at times be challenged, since the Enemy does not want you to succeed for God's cause.

Therefore it is written: "For to this end we both labor and suffer reproach, because we trust in the living God, who is the Savior of all men, especially of those who believe. These things command and teach. Let no one despise your youth, but be an example to the believers in word, in conduct, in love, in spirit, in faith, in purity. Till I come, give attention to reading, to exhortation, to doctrine. Do not neglect the gift that is in you, which was given to you by prophecy with the laying on of the hands of the eldership. Meditate on these things; give yourself entirely to them, that your progress may be evident to all. Take heed to yourself and to the doctrine. Continue in them, for in doing this you will save both yourself and those who hear you (1 Timothy 4:10–16)

You see, a disciple has a very connected heart with God; he knows what is so important. There is a purpose we are blessed with, a gift to be used and not neglected. The greatest gift is to help others.

We should be bold and spread God's revelation for the End Times. If we read and understand what is going to happen, we will know what to do and will be prepared to save ourselves and others as well.

When you do the work of God, you will have challenges from the Enemy. This is a good sign that you are on track with God and will keep fighting the good fight through all God's tools.

When things are too easy and you are not facing adversity, then chances are, you are heading in the wrong direction, and the Enemy won't stop you until you enter the den of wolves.

Do not let your hearts be hardened; rather, finish the race with steadfast faith, doing all you can.

All my life I have had a Christian heart, and I studied the Bible from a very early age. On many occasions, the Enemy and his demons have attacked me. I recall an incident in my early teens. Two old men walked past me and called me Frankenstein for no reason. Immediately, I remembered a verse from the Bible. Jesus said in Matthew 10:22, "And you will be hated by all for My name's sake. But he who endures to the end will be saved."

I cannot begin to express how joyous I was to hear those ugly words from the demons, since this was my proof that I belonged to the most powerful, greatest, loving God. I was hated due to their jealousy. I remember that I skipped, jumped with joy, looked up to the sky, and told my Father how much I loved him.

You see, knowing Scripture allowed me to conquer the Enemy's tactics. He tried to hurt my mind and heart, but I was able to quench the Enemy's darts by using Scripture for my own good.

I don't think seeing me happy made those men very happy, since they were trying to rob joy from me, and I knew this was the beginning of many trials to come. God also said, "Behold, I send you forth as sheep among wolves: be ye therefore wise as serpents and harmless as doves" (Matthew 10:16).

Many Christians now see the times we are in and try to help spread the gospel, but as it is also written, "The harvest truly is great, but the laborers are few" (Luke 10:2). That's sad but true. We see more Christians giving up and keeping silent in their faith. You can't give up and let the Enemy have the upper hand. We see how diligently Satan and his demons work to dismantle and disrupt our own United States

Constitution's rights of free of speech and exercise of religion.

The darkness is in high places, including the government and presidents. The Bible says Satan uses kings to gain control of the rest of us and manipulate the system.

Pastors and priests are now being penalized if they bring politics into their sermons. Jesus's prophecies had very much to do with politics and events that would take place and how they would affect us worldwide.

Jesus warned us of several political powers that are rising and determined to change laws into lawlessness. We can see this is happening rapidly now through the following:

1. Violation of our privacy via e-mails and telephone surveillance as a weapon of control over us
2. Gun law restrictions to defend ourselves, leaving us as sitting ducks in the event of martial law
3. The ridicule and attack of our free speech and Christian beliefs. We are viewed as the bad guys and used as more justification to attack Christianity.

4. Requirements of religious congregations to pay for abortions when this is clearly against their beliefs.

5. The condoning of same-sex marriage, since the U.S. Supreme Court ruled it as a national law.

The abuse of having arms may have caused some forced restrictions, however, especially considering the attacks on Paris and San Bernardino in late 2015. These changes leave open the possibility that Satan and his minions will be able to destroy us because we can't protect ourselves under the Second Amendment.

Through martial law it isn't impossible to see civilians captured. We have seen that other states, such as Texas, have already exercised martial law.

Regarding same-sex marriage, I do believe it's against God's moral law of creation and procreation. However, I have also met many homosexuals who are very spiritual in Christ and have a profound love for Him. I don't believe they have chosen this life for themselves; it is part of a chromosome gene they were born with, so I have to search within my heart for compassion and love for these people. The Word of God says, "For whosoever calls on the name of the Lord shall be saved" (Romans 10:13).

The most important word is *whosoever*. The only requirement is to believe and call on God.

I don't promote homosexuality; I don't believe it is God's ultimate plan, since he created Adam and Eve, not Adam and Steve. But let's face reality. The problem is undeniable when you see children with opposite-sex characteristics.

I don't believe those children planned on being born that way. In fact, I know a man who hated being gay; he had such terrible guilt that he refrained from any intimacy and wished he had never been born. He feared he was going to hell when he expressed he was living with this problem.

I later learned that he died in his sleep.

I recall watching CNN and learning about a teenage boy who was gay. Bullies pretending to be his friends lured him to a remote area, chained him to a fence, threw rocks at him, and mocked him for being gay. They brutally killed this young boy who appeared not to hurt a fly. Maybe this young gay boy believed in God, and those bullies who weren't gay had committed murder. Who do you think would be welcome in heaven? The boy or the bullies?

Sometimes I believe our Christian faith, when used to judge, can turn people away from God. In history God used sinners and transformed them so they did great works.

We must bring love to all people and let God do the rest, for God's understanding is far greater than ours. Isaiah 55:9 says, "For as the heavens are higher than the earth, so are My ways higher than your ways, and My thoughts than your thoughts."

I remember hearing the story of my grandmother coming to America from South America and didn't speak a word of English. She raised four children on her own and got a job sewing. She went to church every Sunday and made all of us go.

She helped the homeless, always giving food whenever she could. Apparently she was a perfect Christian in God's eyes, but she had one major conflict from being a true Christian. She was prejudiced against African-Americans from her upbringing.

I remember once when she was outside her porch as an African-American walked by. She told him to walk across the street as if she owned it. I told myself that she was going to get hurt, but little did I know that God had better plans for her.

My grandmother had an anxiety disorder. When she was upset, she hyperventilated and couldn't breathe. One day, she had an episode, but no one was around to help her, so she walked outside to the street to find help, gasping for air. An African-American who was walking by saw my grandmother in distress. Immediately he went to her aid and gave her mouth-to-mouth resuscitation to restore her breathing.

Could you believe that, out of all people, God brought into her life a man for whom she had preconceived bitterness without any merit?

Not only did he save her life, but he also saved her from condemnation, for God says to love others as we would love ourselves.

Ever since then, she told the family about her experience and realized God had put the man there for a reason. She was so grateful to the man for saving her life and welcomed all African-Americans from that point on. You see, love is the answer. God said to love others as we would love ourselves, since this is one of the greatest commandments.

Luckily, my grandmother listened, repented, and changed her behavior. She is now resting in peace.

The only race we should be concerned about finishing is the spiritual race with love and perseverance, because the Enemy is also in the race to prevent us from finishing it with God.

Any sin that is a weight lying heavily on us will only slow us down. We need to remove any obstacles so we are free to run and have a relationship with God.

Even cyclists in the Olympics shave away tiny hairs so they can move faster. We need to think the same way. Take any opportunity to help someone, make amends, or remove obstacles that are keeping you down.

We have no time to waste. We need to stop casting stones. Let me repeat what Jesus said in John 8:7. "He that is without sin among you, let him first cast a stone." There should be no more blaming, yelling at each other, fighting, or bringing out the worst. Rather we should love, edify, and bring out the best.

If someone you know isn't capable of change, the Bible says that, should a branch produce no fruit, it is best to cut the branch off than to destroy the whole tree.

Sometimes it's okay to walk away if a situation is unhealthy, for we can always pray for someone. This is where I feel we have a loving God whose understanding is far above ours. He has more compassion and is more loving than we are.

Jesus forgave an adulterous woman and said to sin no more. For those who have made a personal choice and refused God as their Creator just like anyone else, going their own way without repentance, there is condemnation and judgment.

As a Christian I don't promote same sex relationship especially for people who use perversion to tempt those who are heterosexual into behavior that is unnatural for them. We have seen this problem even inside Catholic churches, with priests manipulating little boys. This is the work of the Enemy, and for them, there is no hope but condemnation should they refuse to repent and change their ways, but time is extremely short.

For it is written, "The Lord is not slack concerning His promise, as some count slackness; but is longsuffering to us, not willing that any should perish, but that all should come to repentance" (2 Peter 3:9).

God loves us and has given us plenty of time to find Him and warn others, because He wants all of us to be saved.

Is it not loving to tell your child not to cross the street without looking first so he or she doesn't get hit by a car?

Is it not loving to tell your child not to put his or her hand in hot water or it will get burned?

God doesn't want us to be left behind, so he gave us revelations to reveal the truth so we can see both ways, know what is coming ahead, and avoid getting burned in the end.

Over the years we can see how drastically our world has deteriorated from the loss of great men in political power—from Abraham Lincoln for the human rights movement, condemning slavery; to Martin Luther King, bringing God as the Supreme Judge and not man; to John Kennedy, a devout Christian who was against any secret society, believing all works must be transparent for the people; and to Ronald Reagan, who was the first president to propose a Constitutional amendment on school prayer. All these great men were Christians.

Have we seen any presidents assassinated (or attempted) for being a bad president? No, only the good ones, I have noticed.

During our American history, we had principles, morals, and values—and our country was great. Evil has systematically destroyed our very foundation of what this country was built on: to trust one nation under God.

Satan's goal is to replace godly principles and trample our very core to lawlessness. In today's world, we see that our president, Barack Hussein Obama, once elected, didn't waste any time announcing that America is no longer a Christian nation. Our Commander in Chief interviewed with a famous YouTube woman, who eats Fruit Loops from a bathtub, rather than meeting with Prime Minister Netanyahu of our beloved Israel. Netanyahu is fighting with his country against Iran's continued threats to blow up Israel and America.

This is how severely our nation is being forced to ignore God's commands. God says in Genesis 12:3, "And I will bless those that bless you, and curse him that curses you: and in you all families of the earth be blessed."

We are in the process, for those who agree with the evil powers of government will also taste the same wrath, and we will have no one to blame but ourselves.

We must remove the blinders from our eyes, as the only thing that can change is our choice in what principles we support, but we can't change God's plan. God said, "The first was like a lion and had the eagle's wings. I watched till its wings were plucked off, and it was lifted up from the earth and made to stand on two feet like a man, and a man's heart also was given to it" (Daniel 7:4).

Yes, this is in reference to the great United States of America. We are going to fall hard and sudden, within one hour, as described in the fall of the mysterious Babylon. So we can see the concern regarding Israel's prime minister Benjamin Netanyahu. He is striving to forewarn against Iran's attempt to gain nuclear weapons of mass destruction. This is a real threat not only for Israel but also for Westerners.

We know we are headed for trouble when we see President Barack Hussein Obama is determined to negotiate with Iran regarding their nuclear program in some kind of treaty with limited restrictions, when many sources say any negotiations with Iran, the capital of terrorism, is a bad one.

Former New York City mayor Rudy Giuliani also stated on Fox News that these negotiations wouldn't prevent Iran from obtaining a nuclear weapon within ten years.

Let me now address all Obama supporters. If you disagree with this view, that's okay, and I do not mean to offend you. The most important message comes from our Redeemer, Jesus Christ, as no one knows when God will call on you. Hopefully your house will be in order when you meet him. For many who have been called to be a witness to God, understanding the Bible is very political, and my attempt is to put political aspects in today's biblical reference so you can be equipped to know where we are headed.

Regardless of what has happened yesterday or will happen tomorrow, our focus must be to be ready and be right with God today, for the time is coming when we are not supporting our allies and what this nation was built on. We will no longer be "one nation under God." Instead, we will go after our own desires—politics over principles—and turn a blind eye over to rhetoric of the government, which has seriously influenced the media, education, and politics, leaving God out of the picture.

We listen to the media, but do we stop to think about how many issues are in reference to what God said would happen? The media sure won't tell us. Why not?

We are not equipped and prepared, so we keep our focus on fear rather than on faith.

The Bible says, "Hypocrites! You know how to discern the face of the sky, but you cannot discern the signs of the times?" (Matthew 16:3). This means we can predict the weather, but we can't see that what is happening around us is God's revelation happening before our very eyes.

Of the several news network personalities available to us, I happen to like and respect Sean Hannity the most. He has integrity, is bold, perseveres, and is not afraid to discuss challenging issues that are not popular. He will go against political and foreign agendas if they compromise our constitutional rights, and he is a strong advocate. He fights for us and will not waver to do good even at all costs.

Sean Hannity even visited Israel during a very dangerous time during a war with the Palestinians.

He exposed tunnels Palestinians use with the intent to capture and kill Israelis. Sean put his own life at risk to help us understand the challenges Israel faces each and every day.

Israel, of course, is concerned with the nuclear program. Iranians designed it for themselves as they pray and chant to blow Israel off the face of the map, but they also pray and are determined to get rid of the United States. They see Westerners as the Great Satan and Israel as the Little Satan, and you can bet that nuke has the name of the United States all over it.

So what does President Barack Hussein Obama do? He announced on July 14, 2015, that he and his administration had achieved the Iranian nuclear deal, which is called the Joint Comprehensive Plan of Action. It would lift sanctions that have crippled Iranians financially for over a decade, preventing them from having financial power and obtaining a nuclear bomb and ballistic missiles.

Israel's prime minister Benjamin Netanyahu responded and said on Fox News, "This is a stunning historic mistake as Iran continues to chant the destruction of America and Israel." This agreement favors our enemies, who have killed Americans and chant to destroy America and Israel. Sadly, not only did Barack Obama make a deal for Iran to obtain ballistic missiles of mass destruction, which could reach the United States. He also unfroze their financial resources, which his predecessor, George W. Bush, had frozen with the United Nations after the 9/11 attack. Lifting those sanctions enables Iran now to obtain over $150 billion, giving them financial power to purchase military equipment and ballistic weapons. Now they can afford uranium enrichment, which they have nearly completed for their nuclear bomb.

Iran is one of the smartest countries in the world when it comes to operating in a covert manner. We don't have all the intelligence to know what nuclear capabilities they have already in place in their vast territory.

This nuclear program deal was designed with the pretense to delay their nuclear program over the course of ten years; however, this administration did nothing to prevent the extremist fringe determined to destroy United States and Israel. In fact, a day after this agreement was reached to give them more than $150 billion, Iranians chanted, "Death to the United States." Let's face it: they cannot be trusted. And to make matters worse (and why this is such a bad deal), one of the requirements in this nuke deal was that Iran would allow inspectors to view their facilities, requiring a twenty-four day advance notice.

It shouldn't be rocket science to imagine how many "undeclared" facilities they have as well as undeclared underground tunnels. If Mexican drug lord El Chapo could escape and develop an underground tunnel right under the Mexican prison, which had lights, air-conditioning, and a motorcycle to boot, for his escape right below the high security of the government's noses, what makes anyone think Iranians, the leaders of terrorism, cannot build and hide nuclear programs in their own back yard?

If there was nothing to hide, it should be mandatory to request inspections on all their facilities, especially if we are giving them billions of dollars and putting our generation at an extremely high level of risk. We virtually gave them a bomb at our expense and paid them to bury us. It's just a matter of time, but it will happen. The Iranians have already violated the nuclear agreement, since it was reported that they already tested a long-range missile. This negotiation is designed for defeat, not victory.

Just in the same way that we taught al-Qaeda to fly our own airplanes, they turned around and used our own planes against us, killing almost three thousand souls.

All these negotiations with Iran were clearly and strongly advised against; however, President Barack Hussein Obama, with his administration and the United Nations, tries to convince the people that this deal is the best option.

President Barack Hussein Obama has made Iran richer and stronger, and with ISIS as the richest terrorist group combined, they will be unstoppable, as both chant, "Death to America and Israel."

After Obama's announcement liberating Iran's sanctions, the Iranian leader Ayatollah Khamenei announced that they will continue to defend their allies, Syria and Hezbollah. They continued to say that should they go to war with America, the Iranians will not be humiliated, emphasizing that war will not end their hostility toward the United States and Israel, since Iran continues to support and fund terrorism.

The supreme leader of Iran publicly announced their success and denounced Israel's failure to try to stop this deal while they continued to chant about death and destruction to America and Israel.

To make matters worse, any deal would be a bad deal with Iran, but in good faith, the president, Barack Hussein Obama, didn't even negotiate the release of the three U.S. hostages and one possible hostage of unknown location.

American Christians are held as hostages in Iran, and President Barack Hussein Obama in his defense said that negotiations would set a precedent, allowing Iran to ask for more sanctions to be lifted.

Some have reported that Iran needed this deal more than the United States; if that's the case, then releasing Americans hostages should have been easy to negotiate. Iran reportedly requested the ballistic missile sanction to be lifted as well, even though this wasn't part of the deal.

President Obama gave it to them. This would have been the perfect opportunity to request the release of American hostages, but Obama gave it to them anyway. However, he released five of the worst terrorists in exchange for one sergeant, Bowe Bergdahl, in late 2015 faced a court-martial on charges of desertion and misbehavior before the enemy.

I have spoken to several Iranians about this deal to learn about the consensus of the Iranians; they expressed even more concern than the liberals, stating that this is the worst deal that could happen to America.

These are the Iranians who left Iran after the revolution when the Ayatollah Khamenei came into power and turned Iran into a terror communistic country. They continued, "You cannot trust the supreme leader Ayatollah of Iran, and for Obama to make a deal with us, President Obama must also be a different kind of terrorist to destroy your own country."

It's not difficult to see that this is the direction we are heading; it's also prophesied in the Bible. " For in one hour such great riches came to nothing.' Every shipmaster, all who travel by ship, sailors, and as many as trade on the sea, stood at a distance and cried out when they saw the smoke of her burning, saying, 'What is like this great city?" They threw dust on their heads and cried out, weeping and wailing, and saying, 'Alas, alas, that great city, in which all who had ships on the sea became rich by her wealth! For in one hour she is made desolate.' " (Revelation 18:17–19)

I believe this will be that final day the Enemy has been waiting for. The great United States of America, that great city, will go up in smoke within one hour, because we have forgotten what this country was built on: "In God We Trust."

We have become a nation of greed and gluttony as well as the capital of pornography and drugs. Alcohol abuse is prolific, and sexual abuse and other carnal sins separate us from God. The gift of this great nation He has given us has been irresponsibly abused.

As a child, I remember reading Revelation and being horrified about the events that are going to take place, especially the capture of Christian people and their being beheaded for their faith. I thought, *Who does beheadings in this day and age? How can this happen? What kind of man or power can kill massive people around the globe?*

Honestly, I knew it was coming but just not this soon.

As I turned on the news and heard about the first beheading of our journalist James Foley, I said, "Here it is! Here is the conception of birth pains before it gets worse."

In the Bible, the word *Armageddon* appears only once, in Revelation 16:16. The word in Hebrew is

Har Megiddo. Har means "strong," and *Miggido* means "mountain or a place of gathering."

As we can see, people from all over the globe are flocking to join ISIS, this strong army. ISIS is a fundamental, radical Islamic group that seeks a world in which Islam is the one true religion and everyone else is an infidel that must be destroyed. They are meeting at boot camps (hidden deep in the mountains), training, and preparing. ISIS is becoming bigger and stronger.

The characteristics of the Middle East, those taking place now, are described prophetically in the Bible.

ISIS is nothing more than a distorted, twisted offshoot of Islam. Its purpose is to commit horrendous, barbaric war crimes to wipe out Christians and other faiths that do not align with their demonic ruler. This will not go in vain by our God.

Jesus warned us about the coming Armageddon and the supernatural powers that will fall soon after his people are killed. The wrath of God will come as has never been seen since the conception of earth.

You see, all Christians who are being beheaded for not bowing down to ISIS are in heaven now, in peace and serenity.

There are more birth pains to come before the second coming, since this is a process. ISIS is methodical, systematic, and cunning, with the characteristics of its evil ruling spirit, Satan, guiding it. The Bible says, "For they are the spirits of devils, working miracles, which go forth unto the kings of the earth and of the whole world, to gather them to the battle of that great day of God Almighty" (Rev. 16:14).

The Bible also describes how Armageddon will originate in the Middle East. ISIS was born right in the heart of the Middle East, and it is preparing to gather and conquer other countries.

The Iraq War had made it possible for them to expand once President Barack Hussein Obama moved our troops out. His predecessor, George W. Bush, had tried to liberate Iraq and lost many of our American soldiers in the process, leaving our weapons behind for this terror group to confiscate. These weapons gave them manpower to use against their own civilians.

ISIS has significantly increased in numbers, beheading, killing, and brutally torturing thousands of innocent people. Many of them are Muslims, Christians, old and young men, woman and children.

The Bible also says, "Their bows also shall dash the young men to pieces; and they shall have no pity on the fruit of the womb; their eye shall not spare children" (Isaiah 13:18).

We know ISIS has captured children from their parents and killed them. ISIS's followers have even beheaded children and put them up as trophies on sticks. They clearly have no pity or mercy of any kind; they are barbaric beasts.

Revelation 6:11 says, "Then a white robe was given to each of them; and it was said to them that they should rest a little while longer, until both the number of their fellow servants and their brethren, who would be killed as they were, was completed." This is a spiritual war and there is no stopping it; ISIS will grow only until they have wiped out every religion and created a new world order under their regime as they march to their final destination, the final battle, to fight Christ himself.

The Bible says that in the End Times, Christians are expected to go through these tribulation periods while we are in the final battle with Satan and his demons.

Yes, even Barack Hussein Obama, who is in the highest seat of political power, is a huge contributing factor in fulfilling the End Times.

Allowing very minimal support to the civilians in the Middle East from this group of radical Islamic terrorists only allows them to spread to the point that the battle at Armageddon will be uncontrollable and devastating to mankind.

To make matters worse, President Barack Hussein Obama released five of the most dangerous terrorists, one of whom was in charge of leading al-Qaeda. Another was directly involved in the 9/11 attack in New York City.

This is unacceptable. Barak Hussein Obama was very aware of ISIS prior to our having any knowledge of it, so to release five terrorists bent on destroying America makes no sense to me. However, God does say in Matthew 7:16 that we will know who someone is based on the fruits of his or her labor, so let the actions speak for themselves.

As President Barack Hussein Obama tries to now divert our attention to this catastrophic dilemma from ISIS, to minimize them and give the perception that they have been contained, we will soon be suffering from this consequence, as many of the countries are now crying for help to be rescued as ISIS continues to grow.

The great United States has always had a superior military force to handle such aggressive militants, but our military has virtually been cut in half. We don't provide real interventions or solutions for our national security, while innocent citizens are being slaughtered at a massive scale.

Here is more proof that ISIS is growing out of control, causing thousands to flee those countries. This is proof I personally witnessed.

Recently I was on Princes Cruises ship in the Mediterranean Sea bound for Istanbul Turkey. The ship received a mayday call from Athens Greece Coast Guard that there were six stranded sailboats distressed field with Syrian refugees including small children. Greek officials asked Princess Cruises to pick them up as it appeared their boat was in distress and to rescue them.

There were about one hundred refugees left with nothing, and they had left everything behind to save their souls. Because of high levels of security, Princess

Cruises had to call out children services, security, and the Red Cross to ensure safety for everyone.

Everyone on the ship was delayed a day to their vacation destinations, but most people understood and were compassionate about the circumstances.

The private sector—from individuals, not the government—paid the heroes who rescued them. People helped to rescue them when our own government failed to stop ISIS and the ensuing refugee crisis. You won't hear this story on the news, since it is uncensored to show just how bad it is for civilians and to describe the devastation they are in. We might not see the real threat ISIS poses on the globe until it is too late and its mission has succeeded.

People are fleeing by the hundreds of thousands, leaving everything behind and running for their lives. Italy and Greece are two of the closest countries near the region. They are flooded with refugees, and we don't know how many ISIS followers are with them.

It is very clear how serious this situation is for families trying to escape genocide. It is incredible for President Obama to use diversion tactics to minimize ISIS as a "JV team," when the ISIS agenda is to grow and make the Holocaust look like the JV small league.

Citing climate change as the global national security threat to mankind as opposed to ISIS, our real threat, is incomprehensible.

What is wrong with this picture? Do we think our president is unaware of this eminent threat? Of course he's not; he receives the highest level of intelligence about gruesome killings we are not privy to. He is not stupid, but I think he thinks we are.

While we focus on climate change, which of course is a great concern, it isn't as critical as our national security threat from this group bent on global genocide.

It is no secret that ISIS is hijacking innocent people, oil refineries, and countries. It is becoming stronger and larger; in fact, it is the richest terror group in history, a true untamable beast. They get off on televising their heinous crimes for the world to see; they have no fear and claim their victims' heads as trophies.

This, in my view, is the beginning of Armageddon, for they will march in armies, and their means of killing is exactly how the Bible prophesied it would be: by beheading. Is that fact coincidental?

Absolutely not. It couldn't be any clearer. God said this is what they would do, and it's exactly what they are doing in the twenty-first century. Many who have joined forces with ISIS are intrigued; the Bible also states that many will be intrigued by a False Prophet (in this case, ISIS) and be brainwashed into joining them.

Their propaganda, which says there is a much higher cause, is intended only to lure those who never knew Jesus and have no other purpose to live for in their lives. These are lost souls who will find their final destination as burning in torment forever in hell.

The Bible says, "But these, like natural brute beasts made to be caught and destroyed, speak evil of the things they do not understand, and will utterly perish in their own corruption" (2 Peter 2:12). It also says, "While they promise them liberty, they themselves are slaves of corruption; for by whom a person is overcome, by him also he is brought into bondage." (2 Peter 2:19).

I believe this little verse in the Bible explains ISIS well. This terror group and its followers are beasts, another word for animals, with teachings they don't understand; they believe they are fighting a just cause and will be liberated because they are under the spell of the False Prophet. This situation will end up destroying their lives when they learn the hard truth of Jesus Christ, whom they are waging war against.

The ruler, of course, is Satan himself. He drives his many demons into this spiritual warfare; however, many are lost souls who became part of their environment. They are not educated, nor have they accepted Jesus Christ, so they do not question any consequences of their actions. For God also said we should pray for our enemies, as when the Roman armies crucified Jesus. he prayed for them, saying, "God forgive them for they not know what they are doing." (Luke 23:34)

I feel that many of these lost souls have joined ISIS; indeed they don't know what they are doing. Many are young and strongly influenced by manipulators, demons, haters, who twist the Islamic faith into a work of righteousness, and as written, they think they will be liberated.

God said in 2 Corinthians 11:14 that Satan disguises himself as an angel of light, but he is darkness.

The army of ISIS has now grown in considerable numbers; many have tasted death and have fierce adrenaline for more as they parade the streets, raising their fists and their artillery, demanding praise and worship from their followers.

This isn't a true Muslim war, since many Muslims are being slaughtered brutally for their belief in the Koran. The Koran acknowledges Jesus as a prophet rather than the Son of God, but it does teach about a God who is most loving and forgiving.

The Koran says, "It is they who rejected the communications of their Lord, and the encounter with Him. So their works are in vain. And on the Day of Resurrection, We will consider them of no weight." (Chapter 18, Verse 105)

This is a new breed. This is a spiritual war against Christ, his people, and anyone believing in God who is full of grace and forgiveness. They are the antichrists, and Armageddon is here!

We are fighting evil; Armageddon is another word for an organized, strong terror group, which is the size of a great army.

God also prophesied that Satan will not only lead them but also give the False Prophet his seat. There are many false prophets, but we can clearly see one in ISIS leader Abu Bakr al-Baghdadi. He preaches a false doctrine of life after death, and he teaches the killing of innocent people to save their souls when they are being led into an eternal furnace of fire.

There couldn't be a greater false prophet than this. He teaches to destroy, to brutally kill, and he burns mothers with their children alive. He also preaches the beheading of our brothers and sisters.

When we begin to see the battle at Armageddon grow in historical numbers and America collapse, Satan will be revealed once he knows his dominion has control of the people.

You see, Satan is very cunning; he won't reveal himself suddenly and possibly lose this war, since he knows it's a numbers game. We are still in control; that's why he hasn't yet appeared, and he's using his False Prophet to do all the dirty work first.

Once the False Prophet has succeeded in numbers and gains control (we see False Prophets now controlling Syria and Iraq, which are very large countries) and has wiped America off the face of the earth, it will be much easier to control the remaining countries. They are already scattered in huge numbers in America, Europe, Africa, Asia, Egypt, Libya, Pakistan, and everywhere.

As the Bible mentions Armageddon only once, there is great significance in that chapter of Revelation regarding ISIS, which will strike terror and is specific to the End Times.

There will be no more history repeating itself. This will be the final battle, which all of us have suffered since the beginning of our ancestors.

Knowing we are at the last stage means it is crucial that we have our house in order with God. There are no more chances, which is why Armageddon is mentioned only once, but repentance is mentioned over and over again.

What is far more important is that we are saved than those fighting against us will only lead them into their own destruction. Once the door is shut to repentance, it is shut forever.

So we need to know what it is we have been told to do and to remember to do it. The Ten Commandments was created to keep us on the right track, to be safe and not spiritually dead and to be alive and have a joyful relationship with God.

As hard as these guidelines may sound in today's society, they are truly intended for our edification; they keep us spiritually clean with God. We all are without sin, which is why we are continually asked to repent and fight the Enemy, since he will always find something to persecute us with.

A disciple asked Jesus, "Which of the commandments are the greatest of the law?" Jesus answered.

1. "You shall love the Lord thy God with all your heart, and with all your soul, and with all your mind" (Matthew 22:37).
2. "You shall love your neighbor as yourself" (Matthew 22:39).

You see, love fulfills the law, as God is love. "God so loved the world, that he gave his only begotten Son, that whosoever believeth in him should not perish, but have everlasting life" (John 3:16).

Our faith in Christ is the key to eternal happiness, which is soon coming for all to see.

Satan works diligently to destroy and wipe out any remembrance of God's Word and His commandments with the goal to utterly destroy us.

The more he can remove or rob God's Word from us, his image, the weaker we become and are more easily deceived into the lake of fire, which is his ultimate plan.

Satan knows he can't beat God, but he doesn't let his followers know that. Through his lies he has deceived the whole world, those who are not written in the Book of Life.

The Dragon (another of Satan's names) has fierce anger against God for dumping him out of Paradise, and God has injured his ego and pride, which is sin; Satan is going after God's people to devour them. "And because lawlessness will abound, the love of many will grow cold." (Matthew 24:12). Wickedness will increase significantly at a rampant pace. In addition to the Supreme Court declaring same-sex marriage is the law of the land, the Supreme Court of Oklahoma ruled to tear down the Ten Commandments monument placed at the capitol building due to a violation of religious purposes, even though our founding fathers built this country to be "one nation under God." These changes are now turning "one nation" into lawlessness. That monument is now in storage.

We can see that Satan is using government to break down God's principles piece by piece.

The lawless one is attacking the Christian faith. This is a sign of the End Times.

God's revelation is happening now, as predicted; we are witnessing horrific acts. It should be no surprise to know what is coming, and it won't be long until a new world order is established: the End Times. God wants us to be prepared and repent so we will be partakers when His wrath comes, wrath that has never taken place since the conception of the earth that God created.

What will soon be taking place is the fall of the mystery of Babylon, which many believe to be the papacy.

In my view, I do believe Rome is one of "the great harlot that sits on many waters" (Revelation 17:1). The papacy has violated many of God's commandments, and Satan has made its home there to deceive many away from God's teaching.

Let's name a few of God's commandments and look at how the Catholic Church has contradicted God's Word.

1. Exodus 20:4 begins, "You shall not make for yourself a carved image." What does the Catholic Church practice? They have graven images of the cross, saints, prophets, and the

Virgin Mary. Also people go there to kneel and worship. This practice is clearly a violation of God's commandments, as God is a spirit, and we should worship him only as he said. "You shall not make anything to be with Me—gods of silver or gods of gold you shall not make for yourselves." (Exodus 20:23).

2. "Do not call anyone on earth your father; for One is your Father, He who is in heaven." (Matthew 23:9). What do we call a priest? "Father." But there is no Father except God himself. To proclaim that one other than God is specifically called Father violates against God's command. This is an example of Satan planting seeds to arouse God's anger.

3. "Remember the sabbath day, to keep it holy" (Exodus 20:8), for God created the heaven and earth and rested on the seventh day. So what did the papacy do? It changed the Sabbath day from Saturday to Sunday; again, this is another violation of God's commandments.

4. We call the pope the "Father, his Holiness." But what does Jesus say? "for all have sinned and fall short of the glory of God" (Romans

3:23). The pope isn't holy; he is a man who practices falsities against God's commandments. The pope is one of the many false prophets. Remember Pope Benedict XVI? When I looked at him, I thought of Matthew 6:22: "The lamp of the body is the eye," meaning the eye is the window to the soul. And it was astonishing to see millions of people watch Pope Francis as he made a historic trip to our country, which included an address before a joint session of Congress. Hearing the name *Jesus* shared in the media was incredibly refreshing, but I never heard the pope refer to Jesus in the entire address; it seemed more like a political speech about immigration and globalization. Nor did I ever hear the word *repentance*. Remember what James 2:10 says. "For whoever shall keep the whole law, and yet stumble in one point, he is guilty of all."

Although there are many good priests who practice God's teachings and help the less fortunate, at the same time they contradict God's commandments. We cannot twist sound doctrine with falseness. We must be wise and true to God's Word and not follow or worship the pope or man's traditions.

As we can see, clearly the Roman Catholic Church promotes false teachings against the Word of God. We must repent for violating any of God's commandments and committing fornication, as this behavior represents dishonoring our husband, and in the end we are called to be the bride to God. To go outside the marriage is fornication and adultery in a spiritual sense.

But Rome isn't the only harlot, as the Bible explains; the harlot includes many people, multitude, nations, cultures, and tongues. The description of the harlot during the End Times also fits the United States of America, for it is written, "And the ten horns which you saw on the beast, these will hate the harlot, make her desolate and naked, eat her flesh and burn her with fire. For God has put it into their hearts to fulfill His purpose, to be of one mind, and to give their kingdom to the beast, until the words of God are fulfilled. And the woman whom you saw is that great city which reigns over the kings of the earth." (Revelation 17:16–18) This passage today describes not Rome but the United States.

The United States has fallen so far from God's Word that we have become a greedy nation and the capital of pornography. Among other issues, husbands and wives cheat and commit adultery, we have the highest divorce rate among all nations, and there are also other problems, such as legal gambling, drug abuse, and sexual abuse. Let's face it: to be called a harlot is understandable.

Scripture predicts ten nations ("the ten horns of the beast" from Revelation 17:16) will defeat "the harlot." Iran clearly is one of these nations; the proof is seen by it having a nuclear weapon. This is why I believe the other nations came to an agreement to lift Iran's sanctions, which will eventually fulfill God's Word. The word *desolate*, as described in the Bible, means "empty, inhabited, destroyed, gone, and wiped out." As Iran chants for the total destruction of America and burns the American flag, we see that it would take a nuclear weapon to bring the ultimate destruction they pray and chant for. I wouldn't be surprised if they have several nukes already prepared. To wipe out the United States of America, they will be prepared with the goal of utter destruction. But this attack won't be isolated to only one nation that hates the harlot. We also see Russia, China, North Korea, and Iran, who have nuclear capabilities. They don't particularly respect the United States, and they inwardly hate Westerners.

We are currently living in the tribulation period, and many Christians will be killed, as they are every day around the globe, for their faith. This is why it is so important to repent and call on God, for we don't know the exact hour when the harlot will be blown up in smoke.

Luke 17:27–28 says that just as it happened in the days of Noah, so it will be in the days of the Son of Man.

> They ate, they drank, they married wives, they were given in marriage, until the day that Noah entered the ark, and the flood came and destroyed them all. Likewise as it was also in the days of Lot: They ate, they drank, they bought, they sold, they planted, they built.

Isaiah 47:11 also says, "Therefore evil shall come upon you; You shall not know from where it arises. And trouble shall fall upon you; You will not be able to put it off. And desolation shall come upon you suddenly, which you shall not know."

Possibly Iran already has nuclear capabilities, but from Scripture we can see that the world is headed in that direction. Whatever the case may be, this attainment will take place, and the only thing we should concern ourselves with is our relationship with God, since this life is temporary as opposed to everlasting.

As for those who will be present during the destruction of the harlot, I would rather be blown up than experience beheading or other barbaric killings, which many Christians and Muslims have suffered.

Only God knows the number of our days and how His followers will be called; whatever God's plan for my life is, I will stand for Him no matter what.

But even Peter, the disciple of God, told Jesus, "Lord, I am ready to go with You, both to prison and to death." Then He said, "I tell you, Peter, the rooster shall not crow this day before you will deny three times that you know Me." (Luke 22:33–34).

Imagine that Peter saw all of Jesus's miracles of healing and still denied him due to fear of what the soldiers would do to him.

How much harder would it be for us not to deny God should we be faced with similar circumstances? This is why we need to be steadfast in God's Word and believe in him without the shadow of a doubt.

The greatest weapon for Satan is lack of knowledge, and his greatest threats are faith and trust in God.

We see this happening now when ISIS confronts Christians and asks them to either denounce their faith or be killed.

If we aren't right with God or living a godly life, we will have far less chances to stand with God on that great evil day. God highly recommends that we pray to escape, for it is written, "For as a snare shall it come on all them that dwell on the face of the whole earth. Watch therefore, and pray always, that you may be accounted worthy to escape all these things that shall come to pass, and to stand before the Son of Man" (Luke 21:35–36).

To be found worthy describes those who have followed God's commandments, have a repentant heart, and do their very best in God's eyes.

However, many Christians will go through the tribulation, which means they will go through very difficult times, because we are at the end of the rope of darkness.

In one sense it's a fascinating time to be warriors for God, but in another sense we will go through some of the most difficult times of our lives. This is why we need to be more strengthened in God's Word than ever. We will be tested in our faith, even when it comes to life and death.

It's hard to fathom that a love so great would put us through turbulent times, but think of it as the final finale. No matter what, we will do what it takes to stand for God and reject every evil principle that comes our way. We must fight the good fight, even though this fight belongs to God and others hate us for our faith in Him. For the fact that God loves us, we will show our love and loyalty to Him, who is worth every battle of the way.

In return, nothing with God is in vain. In fact, we will rejoice with him in a love we've never known before. Matthew 22:30 says, "For in the resurrection they neither marry, nor are given in marriage, but are as the angels of God in heaven."

Imagine no evil, pain, or suffering of any kind. Even if we had to go through a brief tribulation, knowing it's the end of all evil, God will help us get through it. Because we are living in the dark ages, the time of Satan's last attempt to destroy God's work, Satan will be full force of ultimate vengeance, for it is written in Revelation 2:24 that we don't know the depths of Satan.

Satan knows our weaknesses and will do everything in his supernatural power to target our emotions and break us down to utter hopelessness. If we don't have God's Word in our hearts and minds, he will have the upper hand. It is only through God and our faith in Jesus Christ that we are able to reject his powerful deception of lies.

However, sadly enough, many have fallen away from the Word of God and have given in to the clutches of Satan. They have become his agents, thinking they are doing God's work, but they haven't known the Father.

These are those who have joined ISIS. ISIS believes they are doing God's work in the name of Allah, killing innocent people with severe brutality when they are under the spell of Satan. He leads them through their False Prophet, without having the knowledge of God and the love of our Savior. And because those in ISIS don't know the Father, their followers are easily influenced into believing false doctrine. Satan has perverted their minds for his purpose to destroy God's people. It is also written, "Woe to those who call evil good, and good evil; who put darkness for light, and light for darkness; who put bitter for sweet, and sweet for bitter!" (Isaiah 5:20).

Many ISIS terror groups are co-mingled with lost souls and demons. As those in ISIS hide their faces, the only features exposed are their eyes. But the evil residing in their hearts is easily visible. What may now appear to be a relatively small group will enlarge in catastrophic numbers.

Some theorists don't believe this is the beginning of Armageddon, but according to Scripture, there is no doubt in my mind that this is the spark of the great battle of Armageddon.

When Christians met Jesus in Revelation 6:10-11, they asked the Lord, "'How long, O Lord, holy and true, do you not judge and avenge our blood on them that dwell on the earth?' And white robes were given to them that they should rest yet a little while, until their fellow servants and also their brethren should be killed, should be fulfilled."

This means some time will need to pass for Armageddon to fully evolve and be ripe to test the remaining souls left for the final day of God's wrath.

Until that time ISIS will fill the globe, and many Christians will be beheaded, killed, and tortured for not bowing down to those who worship the Beast.

We also see many Muslims being slaughtered for their faith; they don't condone ISIS as real Islam, because they see it as a perverted version of Islam to further their political agenda. That is because ISIS doesn't follow real Islam; but it is part of Armageddon, another word for an army of terror. Do you think Satan will promote any religion that believes in any God other than himself? No, this is why they are also killing Muslims; there are many peaceful, loving Muslims but not those who follow ISIS in their twisted faith.

However, there are different sectors of Islam just as there are different types of Christianity; there are the Sunnis and the Shi'ites, and both hate each other.

What makes me believe these groups comprise the Beast described in the Bible? The Bible tells us that at the End Times they will fight each other in confusion and kill one another. God has used those who fight against his church to end up fighting each other. We see this happening with both sectors, even though they share the same Islamic faith.

When we see these premeditated, horrendous snuff videos of killing, drowning, and burning people alive, there is no way these are acts of a loving religion and a loving God, who is most merciful and forgiving, as written in the Koran. This is a demonic, evil group filled with hatred. They promote their evil acts through rehearsed propaganda to install terror in the hearts of viewers.

Who else would create videos mocking the deaths of innocent lives but Satan, who uses darkness for good and good for darkness?

There are many demons living on the earth today. As it is written, "Beware of false prophets, who come to you in sheep's clothing, but inwardly they are ravenous wolves" (Matthew 7:15).

They are waiting for the right time to surround us, since that is their strategy, and there will be a time when God will release the remaining demons in hades to kill one-third of the earth. It is written in Matthew 24:15–18, "When you therefore shall see the abomination of desolation, spoken of by Daniel the prophet, stand in the holy place, (whoever reads, let him understand:) Then let them which be in Judaea flee into the mountains. Let him which is on the housetop not come down to take any thing out of his house: Neither let him that is in the field return back to take his clothes."

We see those in Syria and Iraq fleeing to the mountains as ISIS surrounds the city, capturing citizens, but this exodus will occur in a much broader scale around the world. This is when they will all march together, surrounding the cities and snatching people—men, women, and children—for their beliefs. If you accept Christ, you will be killed; and if you reject him, you will be saved in this world only for a short time.

For those who have fled to the mountains, Jesus warns us that strangers on the way will meet us, saying, "Then if anyone says to you, 'Look, here is the Christ!' or 'There!' do not believe it." (Matthew 24:23) We have been warned not to go, for it's only a trap to lure us to kill us, and if we see a home on the mountain hill, knock; and if they refuse to let you into their home, curse the home and go to the next one.

This will be a time of great chaos. People will run from wild men (beasts) as if martial law had fully ripe. The globe is prepared, and they are already here.

God says in Matthew 16:25 and very similarly in Luke 17:33, "For whosoever will save his life shall lose it: and whosoever will lose his life for my sake shall find it."

So if at this hour we are at some point faced with this persecution and taken into custody, we will face Satan's severe persecution. Never reject God to save your life; it's better to lose it and be killed and save your soul with God in eternity.

This is a frightening time, as we already see these horrible acts taking place in the Middle East. This is where it all started, and this is where it will all end. Matthew 10:23 says, "When they persecute you in this city, flee to another. For assuredly, I say to you, you will not have gone through the cities of Israel before the Son of Man comes."

Israel is the focal point and the target, particularly the Holy City. Because Israel is so special to God, it has always been under attack. Sun-Tzu once said, "Keep your friends close and your enemies closer." The Bible says, "I know your works, tribulation, and poverty (but you are rich); and I know the blasphemy of those who say they are Jews and are not, but are a synagogue of Satan" (Revelation 2–9). That means the Jews are also surrounded by demons claiming to be Jews, but inside they have a demonic spirit in human form.

One day I was at a store, and an orthodox Jewish man was in front of me in line, wearing a black hat, short beard, and tzitzit. I could sense he had a very dark spirit. That verse came to mind, and I knew he was a devil and he knew I knew. He turned back to look at me, then left quickly.

Should we see Jews commit a horrendous act, we should revert back to Scripture, remember who they really are, and examine the source. The demons are here, and there are many of them, prepared to go after God's elected people.

This message has the same meaning for the rest of God's people around the globe, those who aren't Jews. Matthew reminds us to beware and not be deceived by wolves in sheep's clothing, waiting to devour souls.

It is also written, "Be sober, be vigilant; because your adversary the devil walks about like a roaring lion, seeking whom he may devour" (1 Peter 5:8).

That time is now here; demons inhabit the earth. The beheadings have now ignited the gathering of armies of Armageddon, and from that point until the rest of the people are killed in the same way.

The question is, for how long is it going to take? It can be a metaphor; Jesus used a lot of these to help explain a situation that hasn't happened yet, but he also explains this way: "Now learn this parable from the fig tree: When its branch has already become tender and puts forth leaves, you know that summer is near: So you also, when you see all these things, know that it is near—at the doors" (Matthew 24:32–33).

We are in the End Times, and the sole purpose of this book is for us to be prepared for the worst. The most important message is to be right with God. Dive into your Bibles, go to church that focuses on God's Word. This is no time to be lazy about this; the more equipped you are with God's Word and his Spirit, the stronger you will be able to stand and face the Enemy at any given time, because God is with you. Satan and his demons have been waiting and preparing to seize this moment, but they are in delusion to think they can win, overthrow God, and be liberated from hell so they can enter heaven.

There will be a time when we are face-to-face with them. My sense is that we will see them for who they are under the sheep's clothing. At that point, they won't hide themselves, and we will be faced with demons for who they are. They will have a very fierce demonic, beast-like appearance, and they will cause as much fear and pain as they can.

But God knows them already, since he and his angels cast them out of heaven. The demons have no power over the angels, but the demons will overcome God's saints. At this point we need to realize that even unto death, this is the last death we will experience, and we will be lifted to eternal life with God. He will take away every pain and suffering we endure for him.

As for the devil, his False Prophet, and the demons, God's wrath has prepared an eternal, burning fire, which is never ending. They will be tormented day and night forever and ever for all the evil they have committed and because they have deceived the whole world and never repented. So again, don't fear their faces.

We see these beasts burning women and children alive because they haven't accepted the demons' image of their god. These women and children will stand for

God and keep their faith, even though they face death. The demons have no mercy and will try any technique to break our faith. If we aren't strong in the Lord, chances are, we will cave to them; the consequences will be eternal punishment, rejecting God for their false one.

It's not worth it, and it's possible to escape tribulation if we repent right now and walk in his commandments, asking in prayer that we escape the things that will pass and be found worthy to stand in front of the Son of Man, Jesus.

As mentioned previously, based on some theories, some believe the mark of the Beast is a chip. It is not, but it's a decision of your deeds, thoughts, and actions by choosing the Devil's image, not a statue. The number of his name is 666, the number of a man, which means to desire things of this world and not to seek the spiritual life God created.

Let's examine what the Devil's image is. Who is Satan, and what does he represent? He is the Father of Lies and is the opposite of God's principles. He lies, cheats, robs, murders, and destroys. He is perverted, selfish, egotistic, and rebellious. He blames and prosecutes. He is the source of carnal flesh and not of the Spirit. He blasphemes God's name, is cunning for wicked gain, and is full of hatred. He is self-absorbed, merciless, and arrogant. He also promotes carnal sin.

Should we live with any of these qualities, we worship the Beast's image, and this is how we receive the mark of the Beast, not God's seal. We will be cast away.

Let's examine God's image. He is loving, forgiving, patient, tender hearted, and righteous. He is filled with sound judgment and is merciful and giving. Of course, he is most Powerful and Omnipotent. He is the first and the last, the Alpha and Omega, and the One True God. There is so much more we cannot understand, as his understanding is far above ours.

We need to examine ourselves and immediately remove any activities that are of the sinful qualities of Satan. We should ask God for forgiveness and depart from them now.

In the end of this book, I have included prayers for repentance and purification. May we ask Jesus to come into our lives so our souls will be saved from the Evil One. This is a bittersweet time, since God says not to let our hearts be troubled. May we look up and know our Redeemer is near. Hallelujah!

At the same time, this is a sad topic, for many of us won't survive the final battle, Armageddon. Only God knows who will be ones left behind, but He says to remain faithful until the end. Should we be captured, we shouldn't premeditate what to answer the oppressors. Jesus says in Mark 13:11, "But when they arrest you and deliver you up, do not worry beforehand, or premeditate what you will speak. But whatever is given you in that hour, speak that; for it is not you who speak, but the Holy Spirit."

After we see the fall of America and the people captured and killed, those who are left will escape to the mountains. Armies from the Middle East will surround Israel, and Satan will stand at the holy temple as a man claiming there is no god like himself. We will then see God's wrath finally come. Revelation 15:7 says, "Then one of the four living creatures gave to the seven angels seven golden bowls full of the wrath of God who lives forever and ever."

At this point, there will be no holding back the wrath of God, and his angels will have his full authority to damage the earth. A full force of supernatural disasters will pound the earth from the heavens. God says he will have the last vengeance, since he has held his peace for those who have witnessed his Word. They will come to repentance and avoid eternal damnation. God's wrath is without mercy to those who have shown no mercy. They will experience pain and suffering like never before. The angels of God have seen the devastation of God's people and have proclaimed to God, saying, "Great and marvelous *are* Your works, Lord God Almighty! Just and true are Your ways, O King of the saint" (Revelation 15:3).

The angels of God are loyal to him, and God has given them power to overcome the earth, each carrying a plague no one can escape. One of the angels will hold the plague to turn all the water into blood, which will represent all the blood they have shed. They will have no water to drink from, and they will see blood everywhere.

Finally, Satan and his False Prophet, who deceive the whole world, will be captured and thrown into sulfur with burning fire, and their smoke will ascend into heaven with their torment day and night forever and ever, and death will have no power, nor sin will be wiped out.

The good news is that the end of evil will finally be put to an end. There will be no more torture, hatred, sadness, resentment, fighting, mourning, or even death.

David, a devoted servant of God, received a divine message from God regarding the fight between good and evil. He was told to send to his people the message regarding the end of days as an inspiration to continue to do good. The Promised Land is coming for his people as well as confirmation regarding the final destruction of the wicked.

Even though Satan and his minions will succeed in their evil plots against God's people, God makes it very clear that this opposition will occur for only a short time. God put revelation in David's heart, and he foresaw exactly what God's people would go through. After receiving this revelation, David responded to God with a sincere devotion to continue for protection in his great love for us.

We see his words are very fitting regarding the evil we see today in ISIS and all evil on the face of the earth, but don't fret. God's people will see the reward of the wicked, evil people. Amen

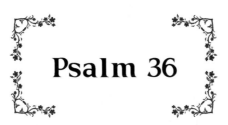

Psalm 36

An oracle within my heart concerning
the transgression of the wicked:
There is no fear of God before his eyes.
For he flatters himself in his own eyes,
When he finds out his iniquity *and*
when he hates.
The words of his mouth are wickedness
and deceit;
He has ceased to be wise and to do
good.
He devises wickedness on his bed;
He sets himself in a way that is not
good;
He does not abhor evil.
Your mercy, O Lord, is in the heavens;

Your faithfulness reaches to the clouds.
Your righteousness is like the great
mountains;
Your judgments are a great deep;
O Lord, You preserve man and beast.
How precious is Your lovingkindness,
O God!
Therefore the children of men put their
trust under the shadow of Your wings.
They are abundantly satisfied with the
fullness of Your house,
And You give them drink from the
river of Your pleasures.
For with You is the fountain of life;
In Your light we see light.

Oh, continue Your lovingkindness to
those who know You,
And Your righteousness to the upright
in heart.
Let not the foot of pride come
against me,
And let not the hand of the wicked
drive me away.
There the workers of iniquity have
fallen;
They have been cast down and are not
able to rise.

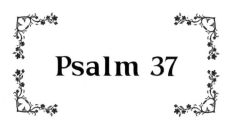

Psalm 37

Do not fret because of evildoers,
Nor be envious of the workers of
iniquity.
For they shall soon be cut down like
the grass,
And wither as the green herb.
Trust in the Lord, and do good;
Dwell in the land, and feed on His
faithfulness.
Delight yourself also in the Lord,
And He shall give you the desires of
your heart.
Commit your way to the Lord,
Trust also in Him,
And He shall bring *it* to pass.

He shall bring forth your righteousness
as the light,
And your justice as the noonday.
Rest in the Lord, and wait patiently
for Him;
Do not fret because of him who
prospers in his way,
Because of the man who brings wicked
schemes to pass.
Cease from anger, and forsake wrath;
Do not fret—it only causes harm.
For evildoers shall be cut off;
But those who wait on the Lord,
They shall inherit the earth.
For yet a little while and the wicked
shall be no more;

Indeed, you will look carefully for his
place,
But it shall be no more.
But the meek shall inherit the earth,
And shall delight themselves in the
abundance of peace.
The wicked plots against the just,
And gnashes at him with his teeth.
The Lord laughs at him,
For He sees that his day is coming.
The wicked have drawn the sword
And have bent their bow,
To cast down the poor and needy,
To slay those who are of upright
conduct.

Their sword shall enter their own heart,
And their bows shall be broken.
A little that a righteous man has
Is better than the riches of many
wicked.
For the arms of the wicked shall be
broken,
But the Lord upholds the righteous.
The Lord knows the days of the
upright,
And their inheritance shall be forever.
They shall not be ashamed in the evil
time,
And in the days of famine they shall be
satisfied.

But the wicked shall perish;
And the enemies of the Lord,
Like the splendor of the meadows, shall
vanish.
Into smoke they shall vanish away.
The wicked borrows and does not
repay,
But the righteous shows mercy and
gives.
For those blessed by Him shall inherit
the earth,
But those cursed by Him shall be
cut off.
The steps of a good man are ordered by
the Lord,
And He delights in his way.

Though he fall, he shall not be utterly
cast down;
For the Lord upholds *him with* His
hand.
I have been young, and *now* am old;
Yet I have not seen the righteous
forsaken,
Nor his descendants begging bread.
He is ever merciful, and lends;
And his descendants are blessed.
Depart from evil, and do good;
And dwell forevermore.
For the Lord loves justice,
And does not forsake His saints;
They are preserved forever,

But the descendants of the wicked shall
be cut off.
The righteous shall inherit the land,
And dwell in it forever.
The mouth of the righteous speaks
wisdom,
And his tongue talks of justice.
The law of his God is in his heart;
None of his steps shall slide.
The wicked watches the righteous,
And seeks to slay him.
The Lord will not leave him in his
hand,
Nor condemn him when he is judged.
Wait on the Lord,
And keep His way,

And He shall exalt you to inherit the
land;
When the wicked are cut off, you shall
see it.
I have seen the wicked in great power,
And spreading himself like a native
green tree.
Yet he passed away, and behold, he was
no more;
Indeed I sought him, but he could not
be found.
Mark the blameless man, and observe
the upright;
For the future of that man is peace.
But the transgressors shall be destroyed
together;

The future of the wicked shall be
cut off.

But the salvation of the righteous *is*
from the Lord;

He is their strength in the time of
trouble.

And the Lord shall help them and
deliver them;

He shall deliver them from the wicked,

And save them,

Because they trust in Him.

A Prayer for Repentance

Dear Heavenly Father,

I come to you today in prayer, seeking
for your Divine Way,
To lead me to your Holy Land where
forever I may stay.
I ask for your forgiveness in all things I
have ever done,
Which have been displeasing to you
and your only Son.
I ask for a new heart, mind, and soul
that reflect your loving Spirit,
That I may walk with you and be
present and coherent,
I no longer wish to walk in my
iniquities,

For it is you I want to praise,

I thank you, Father, for sending Jesus,
your only Son,

Who died for me so I can be with the
Holy One,

I love you, Father, and it is with my
heart, I pray,

That you will call on me on that final
day. Amen.

Prayer for You and Your Family to Escape the Evil Day

Dear Heavenly Father,

I come to you in prayer today, for I
know the day will come,
For the warnings we were given from
Jesus Christ, your Son,
He gave us revelation so we are
prepared,
To live a life of righteousness that we
may be spared,
Yet many Christians will be faced with
great tribulation,

From the Beast and vultures that seek
our total destruction,
You asked for us to pray regarding that
horrible day,
That we may escape these things and be
found worthy,
So with this, I humbly pray for me and
my family,
That we may escape these things
especially on the Sabbath day,
For it is in you, Jesus Christ, who is my
only salvation,
And I thank you for your love and for
sending your revelation.

Amen.

Prayer for
the Globe

Dear Heavenly Father,

We come to you in prayer with sadness
in our hearts,
For the world is divided and split apart,
The hearts of many have grown cold,
Because of the lawlessness many souls
are sold,
Many have strayed and gone their
own way,
Into the snares of the Evil One at the
end of their day,
Your command to love has fallen on
deaf ears,
And nations have wasted so many
precious years,

We pray, O Lord, for all the lost souls
in this spiritual race,
That you may bring them back by your
saving grace,
That they may see the light in their
selfishness,
And come to you in sincere repentance.
Should they fail, for they know not
what they do,
Have mercy, Lord, for our strength
comes from you,
Do not let one of your people be
defeated

But snatch them from the Evil One
into eternity unimpeded,
Lord, please forgive, for your sake, our
God, do not delay,
Because your nation and your people
bear your name.

Amen.

May we all be saved and greet one another in the presence of the Almighty God.

May God bless us all.

Notes

_____

_____

_____

_____

_____

_____

_____

_____

_____

_____

_____

_____

_____

_____

_____

_____

Notes

_____

_____

_____

_____

_____

_____

_____

_____

_____

_____

_____

_____

_____

_____

_____

_____

Notes

_____

_____

_____

_____

_____

_____

_____

_____

_____

_____

_____

_____

_____

_____

_____

_____

_____

Notes